BEST-KEPT SECRETS OF

HAWAII

Publisher and Creative Director: Nick Wells
Commissioning Editor: Polly Prior
Editorial Assistant: Taylor Bentley
Art Director: Mike Spender
Layout Design: Jane Ashley
Copy Editor: Anna Groves

Special thanks to: Catherine Taylor, Dawn Laker, Eileen Cox.

FLAME TREE PUBLISHING

6 Melbray Mews
London SW6 3NS
United Kingdom

www.flametreepublishing.com

First published 2019

19 21 23 22 20
1 3 5 7 9 10 8 6 4 2

Courtesy of **Shutterstock.com** and © the following contributors: 13, 70, 71, 82, 95, 103, 104, 123 MNStudio; 15, 26 Steve Heap; 16 gg-foto; 20, 32, 35 Abbie Warnock-Matthews; 21 Phil O'nector; 22 KEIKOMS; 23 Eddy Galeotti; 25, 37 Chase Clausen; 28, 36 Alfgar; 29 Ingus Kruklitis; 31 Alan Budman; 33 Felix Lipov; 42, 52, 55 Pierre Leclerc; 43 John Orsbun; 44 thetahoeguy; 46 Michael Gordon; 49, 140, 161 Shane Myers Photography; 51 Henner Damke; 53 COULANGES; 56 iofoto; 59 Jeremy Christensen; 60, 170, 171 Joe West; 61 Earl D. Walker; 62 Chris Howey; 63, 66, 74, 76, 164 EQRoy; 65 Manuel Balesteri; 67 Max Earey; 73 Circumnavigation; 75 Douglas Peebles / age fotostock; 80 Raul Bal; 81 LiborK; 83 emperorcosar; 85 andysartworks; 86 David R Nicholls; 87 D.Cz.; 88, 119 Gary Gilardi; 90 Graig Zethner; 90 Theodore Trimmer; 91 Leena Robinson; 92 EastVillage Images; 94 Milaski; 96, 147, 159 Allen.G; 97, 116, 179 norinori303; 98 Elena_Suvorova; 99 Pavel Tvrdy; 100 David G Hayes; 101 Felix Nendzig; 105 Milan van Weelden; 107 Merrilee Holmes; 109 Alberto Loyo; 113 George Burba; 114 Evelyn Jackson; 115 akphotoc; 117 Gambarini Gianandrea; 125 okimo; 128 Norbert Turi; 129 G Ward Fahey; 130, 136 Phillip B. Espinasse; 131 cleanfotos; 132, 158 Leigh Anne Meeks; 133 vasen; 137 majicphotos; 138 LUC KOHNEN; 139 PomInOz; 142 ARTYOORAN; 142 Lifestyle discover; 143 Dlabajdesign; 145, 151 Dudarev Mikhail; 146 AbElena; 149 Jay Bo; 153 David H. Brown; 154, 167 Lynn Yeh; 156 aykfree; 157, 186 MH Anderson Photography; 166 Meadow Todd; 168 kohide; 174, 181 Reimar; 175 Ralf Broskvar; 183 Mike Brake; 184 Benjamin S Fischinger. Courtesy of **SuperStock**: 47, 152; and © the following contributors: 14, 111 Russ Bishop / age fotostock; 19, 45, 50, 57, 93, 176, 182, 189, 50, 57, 93, 176, 182, 189 Stock Connection; 34 Animals Animals; 41 Frank Pali / age fotostock; 58 imageBROKER; 68 Radius; 106 Michael Szönyi / imageBROKER; 110 Nature Picture Library/Doug Perrine; 112 Sonderegger Christof / Prisma; 118 Alvis Upitis; 134 Michael Runkel / robertharding; 150 LOOK-foto; 165 Aurora Photos / Aurora Photos; 169 Masa Ushioda / age fotostock; 172 Douglas Peebles / age fotostock; 173 Photononstop; 177 Michael Runkel / Mauritius; 178 Heeb Christian/Prisma; 180 Jonathan Kingston / Aurora Open / Aurora Photos; 187 Ed Darack. Courtesy of and © 77, 126 Design Pics Inc/Shutterstock/**Rex Features**.

ISBN 978-1-78755-775-8

Printed in China | Created, Developed & Produced in the United Kingdom

BEST-KEPT SECRETS OF

HAWAII

MICHAEL KERRIGAN

FLAME TREE
PUBLISHING

CONTENTS

INTRODUCTION

'For me its balmy airs are always blowing,' said Mark Twain, recalling the months that he spent in Hawaii. 'Its summer seas flashing in the sun; the pulsing of its surfbeat is in my ear; I can see its garlanded crags, its leaping cascades, its plumy palms drowsing by the shore, its remote summits floating like islands above the cloud wrack; I can feel the spirit of its woodland solitudes, I can hear the plash of its brooks; in my nostrils still lives the breath of flowers that perished twenty years ago.' He was speaking in 1889, almost a quarter of a century after his visit to these islands in the far Pacific, but the impressions it had left were as fresh and immediate as they had been on the day they had first been formed.

If it sounds like a dream, a poetic idyll of prelapsarian innocence and beauty, that is because in important ways it is. Crucially, though, it is a dream come true. Hawaii's special, secret quality is that it offers tangible proof of paradise. Those sundrenched, rain-washed forests do exist – we can walk in them. We can bathe in those crystal springs and thrill to the sight of those thunderous cataracts and crashing seas. We can gaze up at those rearing, rocky heights – awe-inspiring and yet never quite menacing – or look out from them across deep and verdant valleys.

Our sense of Hawaii's uniqueness stems at least in part from the impression we have of its splendid isolation. Obviously, it is an archipelago; these are islands. But it is also isolated more radically by its position in the middle of the world's widest ocean, remote from just about anywhere else on Earth. In geomorphological terms, Hawaii is unique: it does not belong to any continental shelf, but sprang up (almost literally) through volcanic action. Each of its islands is a mountain, pushed up over many millions of years by titanic forces far down beneath the ocean bed. Some 3,840 km (2,390 miles) from the US West Coast, it is 6,200 km

(3,850 miles) from Japan; 7,780 km (4,900 miles) from China and 8,500 km (5,280 miles) from the Philippines.

As for the Polynesia with which it is nominally associated, that is every bit as distant. Culturally adjacent and historically connected they may be, but Hawaii is 4,190 km (2,600 miles) from Tuvalu, 5,030 km (3,130 miles) from Tonga and 3,760 km (2,330 miles) from the Marquesas. However, it seems to have been from somewhere in Polynesia that, at some point in the first millennium, Hawaii's first human settlers came, voyaging across the ocean in their wooden outrigger canoes. They brought with them what was already a well-established Polynesian culture. This covered everything from language to land division; from art to agriculture; from social organization to religious values. Over centuries, of course, the Hawaiians would go their own way, their speech and customs very gradually diverging from those of their forebears.

To the first European visitors, who came this way in the eighteenth century, these distinctions did not really register. As far as they were concerned, the Polynesians were all 'savages', whether they were here or in the Marshall Islands. This was not, in fairness, an entirely negative characterization (at least it was not meant to be), for the French philosopher Jean-Jacques Rousseau had popularized the idea of the 'Noble Savage'. This idealized figure, it was argued, had not been spoiled by civilization, so had not learned to lie or cheat, or prize appearances above the simple truth. He was free from the conventions that enslaved more 'advanced' societies. He did not aspire to rank or status or covet material possessions. She (for the 'savage' woman was even more intriguing than her male

counterpart) was not bound by the repressive morality that made relations between the sexes in Europe an area of such suspicion and hypocrisy; she could express her feelings – and offer her favours – as she pleased.

Captain Cook and his crew, arriving off Waimea, Kauai, in 1778 (*see page 33*) on HMS *Resolution* and *Discovery*, found these expectations more or less confirmed. Cook called the place he had 'discovered' the 'Sandwich Islands' in honour of the Earl of Sandwich, an important patron of his explorations back in England. In their utter obliviousness to European-style civilization, the people here were undoubtedly 'savage'. How could they not be? The English and their ships could hardly have been more alien to them. 'In the course of my several voyages,' Cook noted, 'I never before met with the natives of any place

us, that, till now, they had never been visited by Europeans, nor been acquainted with any of our commodities.'

But their lives were evidently enviable in many ways, starting with the eternal summers they seemed to live in, and the apparent endless ease of their existence – a little light fishing and some cultivation apart. Cook's visit was a special occasion, of course, so the visitors did not necessarily see the community on a work footing. Their eagerness to acquire European tools and iron nails (they seem to have been unimpressed by the beads and mirrors Cook's men showed them) should have dispelled any assumptions that their lives were idle and carefree. Even so, scratching a living from the soil here was clearly a lot less difficult than it was in Lancashire or Lincoln; bread (or at least breadfruit, 'ulu) did quite literally grow on trees.

Warm and welcoming hosts, the Hawaiians were clearly bound by strong codes of hospitality. These seem to have governed just about every aspect of their interactions with Cook's men, including the welcome their women gave them. Hawaiians were indeed less sexually inhibited than their European counterparts – or at least so it seemed to eighteenth-century Englishmen. Cook could see that his men were, for the most part, not physically irresistible and wondered at the willingness of Hawaii's women to consort with them. Cook was the product of an industrializing society, schooled in the sort of economic theories so recently set out by Adam Smith in *The Wealth of Nations* (1776), and he concluded that these relations must be transactional, hence the long-standing belief that they were basically trading sex for nails. It seems more likely that, the attitude around such things being quite genuinely much more

so much astonished, as these people were, upon entering a ship. Their eyes were continually flying from object to object; the wildness of their looks and gestures fully expressing their entire ignorance about everything they saw, and strongly marking to

relaxed than it was in Europe, this really was just the women's culturally dictated way of being obliging to their guests.

The idyll ended badly, of course. Having left Hawaii to explore the North Pacific, Cook was killed on his return the following year. He had attempted to abduct Chief Kalani'ōpu'u, on the Big Island of Hawaii, after a row over a stolen boat. In the fight that followed, Cook was killed and his deputy Captain Charles Clerke took charge of the expedition for its voyage home. Meanwhile, it became clear that, along with the now-notorious nails, Hawaii's women had been rewarded with European STDs. The prelapsarian paradise had experienced its Fall.

Cook's visits account for only a few weeks out of a centuries-long history. It is worth dwelling on, though, because this first contact was to shape perceptions of Hawaii in Europe and North America from that time on. And, in important ways, to change the course of a history which was now taking place not in isolation but in dynamic relation with the outside world. If Twain's view of the islands as an earthly heaven speaks to us with enormous eloquence even now, so does his caustic view that Western missionaries condemned those who had the awesome luck to live here to a 'miserable' spiritual struggle, straining for an all but unattainable salvation. Here on Earth, meanwhile, the modernization that the preachers had opened the door to would bring large-scale exploitation, of people and landscape alike, making Hawaii to all intents and purposes one vast plantation.

That door could hardly have remained closed indefinitely, however. Time was never really going to stay still. Easy as it is to see how the monarchy founded by Kamehameha I (*see* page 42)

brought the islands into a rougher and ruder historical era, it at least allowed Hawaii to face the nineteenth century as something like a modern nation state. That, like so many other nations at the time, it came increasingly under the influence of the United States is incontestable and in many ways regrettable – but was it really such a tragedy? Certainly, the Hawaiian story since has had its share of injustice and inhumanity, but the same might be said of any nation's history.

The wonderful thing about Hawaii is the extraordinary extent to which the dream of paradise endures. We can never recapture past innocence. Even so, to visit Hawaii today is still to find ourselves in a sort of paradise, to experience some of that same sense of discovery that was there for Captain Cook.

KAUAI – THE GARDEN ISLE

Even by the standards of the South Pacific, Kauai is strikingly Edenic, its green exuberance as fresh and optimistic as Man's first morning. With its soaring summits, its vertiginous cliffs, its lofty crags and its awe-inspiring waterfalls, we might not unreasonably characterize it as 'rugged' – sublimely so – if its roughest rocky heights were not comfortably clothed in the softest green. Drenched by daily rain, dried off by the blazing sun, its rich volcanic soils bring forth the plenty of the earth. Such was the scene that greeted Hawaii's first Western visitor, Captain Cook, who landed at Kauai's Waimea Bay (*see* page 33) in 1778.

The island makes the perfect starting point for a tour of the islands to this day. The passing of two and a half centuries has brought enormous changes. The primeval idyll is long since over and the islanders must make their way in a much more complex and challenging world. It helps, however, that they have so surpassingly beautiful a homeland. Tourists flock here in their thousands all year round from across the globe and yet, the vast majority of its 1,450 square km (560 square miles) remains substantially unspoiled: a perfect paradise just waiting to be explored.

NĀ PALI COAST

North Shore

Rising sheer out of the sea, the 'high cliffs' (nā pali) that give this coast its name reach heights of 1,200 m (4,000 ft) in places. Access from the landward side is difficult at best: the arduous hike along the Kalalau Trail from the end of Highway 560 and back adds up to a round trip of 35 km (22 miles) over difficult terrain. The effort is certainly worth it, and there's the consolation that the challenges involved in getting there have helped to keep a stunning scene unspoiled.

KĪLAUEA POINT LIGHTHOUSE

North Shore

Situated on a rugged promontory, this little lighthouse, built in 1913, is now a historical monument in its own right. Kīlauea Point's main claim upon our interest, though, is its importance as a National Wildlife Refuge: tens of thousands of seabirds nest here each year. Great frigatebirds, red-footed boobies, tropicbirds, shearwaters and albatrosses all breed, as do rarer species, like the Hawaiian goose also known as nēnē. Higher up the hillside, endangered plants are to be found; below in the ocean, there are spinner dolphins and humpback whales.

HANALEI

North Shore

This little town beside its sweeping bay was once primarily important for its rice paddies and plantations, producing everything from staple roots like yams and taro to breadfruit, coconut, pineapples, bananas, guavas, tamarinds and citruses. Today it is a tourist centre, a picturesque experience in its own right and ideally situated for exploring Kauai's North Shore, and for forays into the island's lush interior. But visitors still delight in tasting the exotic fruits and foods to be found in what remains a major agricultural region.

WAI'OLI HUI'IA UNITED CHURCH AND MISSION HOUSE, HANALEI

North Shore

Its sober green planking a reproach to the more excitable emerald exploding all around it, this church cuts an austere figure against Hanalei's waving palms. Christian missionaries (like those Protestant preachers who ministered here from the 1830s) have come under criticism in recent decades as instruments – whether witting or not – of Western political, cultural and moral imperialism in the Pacific islands. And it is difficult to dispute this role – though at the same time it is arguable that they helped to make an inevitable transition as easy and as painless as it could be.

QUEEN'S BATH, PRINCEVILLE

North Shore

A precipitous footpath takes the visitor down through a descent of 36 m (120 ft) past a waterfall and out on to a lava flow where this pool of fresh water nestles, still and tranquil. The atmosphere of calm can be deceptive. The waves of the Pacific break on the black rocks behind with unexpected force, even in the mildest conditions. Unwary bathers have been swept away (there have been several fatalities over the years) when they have sat to sun themselves on the basin's rocky rim on the ocean side.

'OPAEKA'A FALLS, WAILUA RIVER STATE PARK

East Side/Coconut Coast

The waters of the 'Opaeka'a Stream plunge 46 m (150 ft) over a basalt outcrop before rushing on towards the Wailua River through a deep ravine. The Maalo Road (Highway 583) takes the visitor all the way up the valley to a viewpoint from which the scene, in all its sublimity, can be surveyed. Paradisiacal as the Kauai landscape is in all its greenery, it is easy to forget that it was formed by infernal action: volcanic violence helped to shape a topography of sheer hillsides and vertiginous cliffs.

WAILUA RIVER, WAILUA RIVER STATE PARK

East Side/Coconut Coast

At 32 km (20 miles) in length, the Wailua is Kauai's longest river and the third longest in the Hawaiian islands as a whole. It is formed by two 'forks': the North Fork rising high up on Mount Wai'ale'ale and the South above Hanama'ulu, which come together in a deep and verdant valley. The Wailua is unique among Hawaiian rivers in being navigable in anything larger than a kayak. Here we see an outrigger canoe of a type traditional in the Pacific Islands.

FERN GROTTO, WAILUA RIVER STATE PARK

East Side/ Coconut Coast

Hidden away up the Wailua's southern fork, and only really reachable by boat, the Fern Grotto is one of Kauai's most enchanting secrets. Above, overhanging lava rocks are festooned in maidenhair and sword ferns; below the burgeoning banks explode in tropical reds, pinks, purples, mauves, yellows and greens. The origins of this cornucopia of colour are unexpectedly banal. In the nineteenth century, the area above belonged to a large plantation, whose workers carved out a cistern to collect storm run-off: the trickling of water through these rocks produced this display of ferns.

KAPA'A TOWN

East Side/ Coconut Coast

Once what we might call a 'market town', serving the plantation communities of Kauai's eastern coast, Kapa'a has reinvented itself in recent times. It remains a commercial centre, though, even if its stalls, shops, restaurants and cafés now overwhelmingly cater to tourists. As so often in Hawaii, the dazzling blue of the Pacific sky is picked up in the vibrant colour to be seen in every storefront; every interior; every rack of clothing; every plate of food. Kapa'a is anything but a big and bustling city. It is exhilarating simply being here, even so.

STATUE OF LORD SHANMUGA UNDER THE BANYAN TREE AT KAUAI'S HINDU MONASTERY, KAPA'A

East Side/Coconut Coast

In its maturity, of course, a banyan can come to seem a forest in itself, putting down 'prop roots' that look like the trunks of other trees. A suitably wondrous setting, then, for a figure associated in Indian tradition with the mysterious powers of yoga and spiritual healing. Hinduism first came to Kauai with indentured labourers brought from India to work the great plantations; these days it has all but disappeared. It did, however, leave behind some significant, strange monuments – maybe more intriguing for being situated outside the modern mainstream of island life.

ALEKOKO FISHPOND, LIHUE

East Side/Coconut Coast

This ancient fishpond was created when an 820-m (900-yard) embankment cut off a bend in the meandering Huleia River. Traditionally, it was the work of the Menehune – a mythical race of dwarves who inhabited Hawaii before Polynesian settlers arrived, and who have been celebrated ever since for their reputed craftsman's skills. Whoever brought this fishpond into being certainly knew what they were doing. The dam was built of earth, but faced with tightly fitted slabs of stone, producing a seal which has held for centuries.

WAILUA FALLS, LIHUE

East Side/Coconut Coast

A basalt ledge abruptly ends, the riverbed drops clean away and this twin cataract – one of the world's great waterfalls – results. Thundering impressively in a spectacular cloud of spray, projecting gorgeous rainbows in the refracted sun, the water from this tributary swells the flow of the Wailua River. Claims that the cataract's height is anything up to 60 m (200 ft) are clearly hyperbolic, though the exaggeration is understandable: it certainly seems much higher than its actual 26 m (80 ft). Traditionally young warriors would make the leap into the waters below to prove their courage.

KILOHANA ESTATE, LIHUE

East Side/Coconut Coast

The Wilcox sisters, nieces of the Kilohana Estate's nineteenth-century owner, campaigned hard to keep the historical features of the family plantation after its takeover by the neighbouring Grove Farm Plantation in the 1940s. The entire Kilohana complex has now been preserved as a museum. It is simply full of fascinating exhibits, but the jewel in its crown is the Kauai Plantation Railway. Constructed in the 1880s, this narrow-gauge (762 mm/2 ft 6 in) line was built to haul cut sugarcane from the fields to the mills and refined sugar onward to the coast.

WAIMEA CANYON, WAIMEA CANYON STATE PARK

West Side

Sunshine and showery rain collide in a play of iridescent light above what is popularly regarded as the 'Grand Canyon of the Pacific'. Approximately 16 km (10 miles) long and 900 m (3,000 ft) in depth, this defile was only partly carved out by the eroding action of the Waimea River; geological faulting also played its part. The volcanic peak that forms Kauai seems to have collapsed on its western slopes some four million years ago, leaving this ragged, gaping trench exposed.

RED DIRT FALLS, WAIMEA CANYON STATE PARK

West Side

Kauai may have more impressive cascades, but surely none more arresting than this one. The dazzling white of the sunlit, surging stream set off by the rusty crimson of the canyon's iron-rich earth, this scene seems too vivid in its colour scheme to be natural. Red dirt is a feature of Kauai, in fact – always has been, and its earliest inhabitants adorned their bodies with totemic symbols painted in alaea or 'red clay'.

WAIMEA TOWN (CAPTAIN COOK LANDING SITE STATUE)

West Side

Cook's statue does him no favours here: the explorer looks dull and stolid in bronze, a lovely lei of hibiscus flowers only emphasizing his dourness. Appropriate imagery, some would say, for the impact of a European 'civilization' which has brought the Pacific a joyless legacy of repression, appropriation, exploitation and disease. And yet perhaps it took an outsider's perspective to appreciate the earthly paradise that once existed in these enchanting islands. Despite the destruction, Hawaii remains full of stunning natural wonders.

KŌKEʻE STATE PARK (KAUAʻI ʻAMAKIHI FEEDING ON CHERRY)

West Side

As in other far-flung island groups – most famously Darwin's Galápagos – evolution in Hawaii went its own way. Not just by comparison with the larger landmasses across the ocean but within the archipelago itself, whose islands are in many cases considerable distances from each other. The Kauaʻi ʻamakihi (*Chlorodrepanis stejnegeri*) is a case in point. One of a wider group of honeycreepers (they feed by sucking honey from flowers through their long and slender downturned beaks), it is subtly yet significantly different from related species on the other islands.

KALALAU LOOKOUT, KŌKEʻE STATE PARK

West Side

This viewpoint on the Waimea Canyon Road, 1,200 m (4,000 ft) above sea level, affords unrivalled vistas across unrivalled scenery. 'Vistas' plural, because it is never just a static picture. Coming and going as they are conjured up and then as quickly chased away by the blazing sun, wisps of mist and cloud create a kaleidoscope of shifting light and changing tones. No two experiences of this enchanted valley are the same. The difficult, demanding Kalalau Trail leads down to the Nā Pali Coast, and the kind of views we saw earlier (*see* page 12).

PU'U O KILA LOOKOUT, KŌKE'E STATE PARK

West Side

Opening up panoramic views down the Waimea Canyon, this viewpoint offers the best imaginable impression of what the Nā Pali Coast (see page 12) looks like from the landward side. As so often in Kauai – and in Hawaii as a whole – the colours seem somehow heightened, that much more vibrant than they have any right to be. The red of the rock, the vibrancy of the verdure, the azure of the sea, the white of the ocean foam … all of these are quite thrillingly intense.

MOUNT WAI'ALE'ALE

West Side

Kauai's highest mountain tops out at 1,569 m (5,148 ft) above sea level, but it is not its altitude that is its major claim to fame. It rains here upwards of 335 days a year (in some accounts 360-plus), giving annual totals of up to 13,000 mm (510 in). Hence, of course, the shimmering greenery of its slopes and of surrounding hills. But Kauai's dramatic up-and-down topography makes it a place of microclimates – some leeward mountainside and sheltered valleys end up getting very little rain.

MAUI – THE VALLEY ISLE

All the Hawaiian islands were formed by volcanic action, forced from the ocean bed by unimaginable pressures deep within the earth. The second largest in the group, with an area of 1,883 square km (727 square miles), Maui was originally two separate peaks. One, which rose up 1.7 million years ago, now forms the north-west corner of the island. Its weather-ravaged slopes are deeply scored with ravines and valleys now, so much so that it is hard to imagine that this could have ever been a single massif, and it is generally regarded as a range – the West Maui Mountains.

The second volcano, Haleakalā, was not only a great deal bigger to begin with but it is also much younger, so has suffered much less erosion. Its last eruption was in the seventeenth century and the flows of its successive eruptions spilled across the strait between two islands, fusing them together as the lava cooled and hardened. The low-lying isthmus they produced between the two great mountain masses gave Maui its nickname, the Valley Isle. Though it has seen more economic development than Kauai – first in agriculture and latterly in tourism – vast areas of Maui remain unspoiled.

IAO VALLEY STATE PARK

Central Maui

An eruption of green lushness, gently steaming beneath a sky of blue, the Maui landscape is a picture of fertility and warmth. Often in excess of 70 per cent humidity, moisture is as much a feature as the tropical sun. Fortunately, those same trade winds that bring the rain in such abundance help to keep the island air feeling fresh and cool. Hawaii as a whole, accordingly, is a perfect place for hiking, a lovely wilderness just waiting to be explored.

IAO NEEDLE, IAO VALLEY STATE PARK

Central Maui

A vast volcanic splinter, separated from the adjacent cliffs by faulting and erosion, the Iao Needle is nothing less than a natural wonder. Its sheer scale is striking: it stands 370 m (1,200 ft) tall, rising straight out of the valley floor. Its phallic appearance is unmistakable, and helps explain the reverence it was traditionally held in: for generations islanders saw it as being sacred to Kanaloa, god of the underworld and the ocean. Today it is the tourists who have made the Iao Needle a shrine, a must-see destination for visitors to Central Maui.

KEPANIWAI PARK AND HERITAGE GARDENS, IAO STATE PARK

Central Maui

It is a scene of surpassing calm, the silence broken only by the rustling of the breeze in the lush greenery all around. You would never guess that this had been a place of carnage: this peaceful stream is Wailuku, the 'Water of Destruction', for it was here that the Battle of Kepaniwai was fought, Hawaii's King Kamehameha I prevailing over Kahekili II of Maui. The fight, in 1790, was inconclusive, but Kamehameha the Great was ultimately to extend his authority over the archipelago as a whole, uniting Hawaii as a single realm.

HĀNA HIGHWAY

East Maui

Long and winding and with scores of narrow bridges, it is hardly
a 'highway' as we would normally understand that term, but it
is the only road from Kahului to the town of Hāna. And, given
that its rambling course takes it deep into unspoiled rainforest,
past breathtaking crags, sublime waterfalls and over exposed
outcrops with panoramic sea views, the Hāna Highway is a
hugely popular tourist route. The 'long road' was reputedly built
by Maui's King Pi'ilani in the sixteenth century, but the modern
highway was not completed until 1926.

ALEXANDER AND BALDWIN SUGAR MUSEUM

Central Maui

Sugar was introduced to Hawaii when the first Polynesians
came here in the first millennium AD, but large-scale
cultivation was first undertaken in colonial times. The
plantation here at Pu'unēnē was established by Samuel Thomas
Alexander in the 1870s and, under one name or another, it has
been in business ever since. The modern Hawaiian economy
was to be substantially shaped by sugar: hence the importance
of these antique bottles – beautiful in their sheer ordinariness,
but also a testament to the impact of the industry on every
aspect of daily life.

HĀNA FARMS, HĀNA

East Maui

The town of Hāna grew up in the nineteenth century as a market centre serving the plantations of eastern Maui. By the middle of the twentieth century, the agricultural economy had declined and Hāna was having to reinvent itself as a tourist destination. Like so many other Hawaiian resorts, Hāna has successfully ridden the surfing wave, attracting enthusiasts from far and wide; they have brought their own alternative culture with them. The Hāna Farms have become a popular stop along the Hāna Highway, offering drinks, organic dude-food and whole-earth local crafts.

HAMOA BEACH

East Maui

'The world's best beach', for Ernest Hemingway, who loved Hamoa's air of secrecy, the way its crescent-shaped shore was canopied by overhanging forest trees. At either end, the smoothness of the sand gives way to the roughness of an agglomeration of knobbly lava rocks, so there is a range of contrasting textures. The absence of any offshore reef makes surfing here particularly exciting – and potentially hazardous. Enormous rollers rush straight in here from the ocean. Traditionally they were reserved for royalty; in today's more democratic times, they draw surf connoisseurs from all around the world.

WAI'ANAPANAPA STATE PARK

East Maui

Looking out over a foreground filled with jagged lava rocks, we
see a little bay and, beyond, a tiny black-sand beach completely
crowded on its landward side by thick forest. The name
Wai'anapanapa means 'shining fresh water', and the densely
wooded hillsides here are indeed crisscrossed with streams
and punctuated by pools. It is a lovely place for hiking and for
camping. Lava tubes and waterspouts make for surprising and
spectacular special effects at times; the rocky arches and sea stacks
round the bay are home to important seabird colonies.

KAHANU GARDENS

East Maui

There are prettier places in Hawaii, for sure, but few as
fascinating as this 'ethnobotanical' garden chiefly devoted to
food-plants traditionally grown by the Hawaiians. Here, for
example, we see the fleshy, heart-shaped leaves of the taro,
Colocasia esculenta, whose underground stem was for centuries a
staple for Hawaiians. The long lava platform in the background
is all that now remains of Polynesia's biggest temple, Pi'ilanihale
Heiau, believed to date back more than 700 years. Its precise
religious function is unclear.

HALEAKALĀ NATIONAL PARK (SUMMIT AREA)

East Maui

No trees and no lush greenery here: we might be in another
world in this stark and unforgiving Martian-looking landscape.
Haleakalā, the 'House of the Sun', reaches an altitude of
3,000 m (10,000 ft). This volcano actually makes up a good
three-quarters of Maui's land-mass, but it only really looks
like a volcano on these upper slopes around the summit. The
caldera (collapsed crater) we look across here was traditionally
believed to have been home to the grandmother of Maui, the
island's founding deity.

HALEAKALĀ SUMMIT AND SUNRISE

East Maui

As barren and inhospitable as they may seem, these volcanic
heights had a womb-like role in the birth of Hawaii and a
nurturing influence upon its people. Tradition says that from
here Maui first set out into the sky to lasso the sun and harness
it to light and warm the earth. In geological terms, Hawaii
has barely been born: volcanic action has continued to shape
the archipelago into modern times. For writer Jack London,
Haleakalā was 'the workshop of nature, still cluttered with the
raw beginnings of world-making'.

SILVERSWORD

East Maui

We can say one thing for East Maui – its daisies are
different. Who would have guessed that this extraordinary-
looking specimen (*Argyroxiphium sandwicense*, subspecies
macrocephalum) belonged to the family *Asteraceae*? Really,
though, it is no surprise that so unusual (and unusually hostile)
an environment in so far-flung an island location should have
followed its own unique evolutionary path. Its fleshy leaves,
curving up into a sphere, help the silversword store moisture,
retain heat at this freezing altitude and even focus the warming
rays of the midday sun.

KIHEI BEACHES

South Maui

The beaches may be beautiful, but it is the Hawaiian sky that
steals the show at dawn down here on Haleakalā's eastern coast.
There are miles of beaches around Kihei, every one with its own
distinctive character. Common to all, though, is this irresistible
sense of quiet and calm. And, leafy as the landscape is, the forest
cover is much less dense here. The trade winds, approaching
Maui from the north, have shed most of their moisture on the
island's other side. Here in Haleakalā's 'rain shadow', conditions
are much drier.

MAKENA BEACH STATE PARK

South Maui

Many of Hawaii's most famous volcanoes are 'shield volcanoes' – big, sprawling and for the most part comparatively low in profile, growing up fairly gradually through seeping and slowly accumulating lava flows. (Haleakalā owes its exceptional height to its sheer size.) The volcano we classically read about in our schoolbooks is more strictly speaking a 'cinder cone', formed when ashes accumulate around a blasting volcanic vent. A perfect example, Puʻu Olaʻi – thankfully dormant and luxuriantly overgrown now – overlooks the beaches at Makena, no threat to the swimmers and surfers disporting themselves below.

MOLOKINI ISLAND AND CRATER

South Maui

Makena's Puʻu Olaʻi was traditionally said to be the head of Molokini, a mythic mortal beauty who had stolen a man with whom the fire goddess Pele had fallen in love. Pele, in her volcanic rage, had turned her rival into stone and cut her in two; her shapely body became this curving islet off Maui's south-western corner. Above sea level this story is the most colourful thing about Molokini. However, beneath the crater is an astonishing coral reef, home to over 30 coral species and innumerable exotic fish.

WAILEA BEACH

South Maui

A sandy beach with a large reef, Wailea is a favourite for snorkellers and swimmers. In 2015, high sea temperatures wrought havoc on Hawaii's reefs. Hundreds were left bleached, as corals struggled to cope with the unaccustomed stress. Over 60 per cent of coral species were affected; some reefs lost 90 per cent of their constituent corals. Reefs are living macro-organisms and a great number of Hawaii's died. Since that time, thankfully, there have been signs of a strong recovery – a huge relief not just to conservationists but also to the tourist trade. Scientists are drawing lessons for future crises.

'ĀHIHI-KĪNA'U NATURAL AREA RESERVE

South Maui

Dazzling white against a black background, a cairn of coral stands out amidst the rocks of this coastal lava field below and the gnarled and knotty trunks and branches of the trees above. So dark is the lava that it soaks up solar heat – literally a sun-trap – and raises overall temperatures in the reserve relative to those in adjacent areas on either side. 'Āhihi-Kīna'u, famous for its coral reefs and breeding turtles, is home as well to the Hawaiian monk seal and – further out to sea – the humpback whale.

LA PEROUSE BAY

South Maui

Just to the south of ʻĀhihi-Kīnaʻu, a broad basaltic lava flow has formed what amounts to a peninsula pushing out into the sea. The curving bay it demarcates is an important breeding site for green sea turtles. It is named for the ill-fated French navigator Jean-François de Galaup, Comte de Lapérouse, who surveyed this coast in 1786. He was never to get home to file his reports, however. His expedition disappeared (believed to have been shipwrecked in the Solomon Islands) two years later.

HONOAPIʻILANI HIGHWAY

West Maui

The open road opens up another stunning vista. Hawaii Route 30, more colourfully known as the Honoapiʻilani Highway, extends north and west around West Maui from Wailuku. Hugging the coast through switchback bends, steep climbs and dizzying descents, it offers some of Hawaii's most dramatic mountain and ocean views. Reaching its terminus at Honokohau Bay, right up at Maui's northernmost tip, its course is continued by the Kahekili Highway (Route 340), which completes the circuit back to Wailuku down West Maui's eastern side.

LAHAINA JODO MISSION BUDDHIST CULTURAL PARK

West Maui

Like so many of Hawaii's tourist towns, Lahaina has a subtly alternative feel. It is a good place to come for crystals and reiki treatments, and its 'healing energy' is held in high regard. But its Buddhist Jodo Mission owes nothing to any 'New Age'. Its foundation in 1912 was a response to a more old-fashioned and prosaic problem – that of the Japanese peasants brought to Maui's plantations as indentured labourers. The Reverend Gendo Saito built this complex so that, spiritually at least, they would feel at home.

LAHAINA

West Maui

Halfway up the western coast, the little town of Lahaina has become an important staging post on the Honoapiʻilani Highway. It is also a centre for hikers hoping to strike out into West Maui's mountainous interior, where some of the island's most enchanting scenery – and most fascinating wildlife – are to be found. But Lahaina itself is all urban bustle, a wealth of shops, cafés and restaurants catering to the thousands of tourists who come here every year. Even so, the vibe is easy-going, the mood relaxed; the bright colours of the storefronts speak to Lahaina's irrepressibly upbeat feel.

LAHAINA SUNSETS AND WHALE WATCHING

West Maui

Time moves on and so does tourism. A new generation of eco-conscious visitors to Hawaii is not content to surf, drink cocktails or simply to lounge beside the hotel pool. Lahaina has become an important centre for whale watching. Cruises depart daily, taking eager passengers out into offshore waters to see dolphins, turtles, fish and seabirds – and to watch awestruck as humpback whales like this one breach. Many of the boats have glass bottoms, affording views of reefs and deeps beneath, while some have onboard hydrophones so passengers can hear the whales sing.

PĀ'IA

Upcountry Maui

The surf's always up at Pā'ia, a few miles east of Kahului on West Maui's northern coast. Once a sugar-milling centre, this town has completely reinvented itself in recent years. Its industrial function gone, it has given itself over entirely to leisure. Pā'ia is not, however, for the budget tourist, still less the beach bum of surfing stereotypes. The kids may be content just chasing waves, but their moneyed parents have their sights set higher, browsing and buying art and craftworks in the fancy galleries that abound here.

HO'OKIPA BEACH AND WINDSURFING

Upcountry Maui

This beach not far along the coast from Pā'ia is pretty much the world capital of windsurfing. The winds here, blowing at an all but constant clip, keep the waves nice and choppy and the sails well filled, sending adventurous souls scudding at high speed. To the west is 'Jaws', one of the world's most famous surf-breaks, which sends waves towering to heights of over 18 m (60 ft). But this whole coast is rich in surfing hotspots, thanks to strong and ever-shifting winds and a labyrinth of offshore reefs.

H.A. BALDWIN BEACH PARK

Upcountry Maui

This beach park just to the west of Pā'ia takes its name from one of Maui's most important sugar companies (*see* page 45) who maintained it as a facility for their staff. Since 1963, it has been a public beach. A favourite with locals as well as with visitors, it frequently draws big crowds but it is long and wide enough to accommodate them all with ease. Indeed, generally there's space to spare – even at peak season you can get away from it all at quiet spots like this one further down the beach.

WAIMOKU FALLS

Haleakalā National Park

Through the forests of Haleakalā's far south-west, the Pipiwai Trail runs up from 'Ohe'o Gulch with its delightful rapids and pools past the magnificent 60-m (200-ft) Makahiki Falls. A few kilometres further on the trail reaches its end before a still more stupendous cataract. The Waimoku Falls are estimated to be 120 m (400 ft) high. The exact dimensions scarcely matter, though. It is the aesthetic impact that is overwhelming: the sudden sight of that plume of water plunging down through what seems an oversized arbour of green trees and fleshy ferns.

PIPIWAI TRAIL

Haleakalā National Park

Higher up the Haleakalā hillside, as you make your way up towards the Waimoku Falls, the regular rainforest trees and creepers gradually give way to bamboo thickets. This might be considered a welcome change, and visually perhaps it is. Aurally and atmospherically, though, it is the strangest of experiences walking here. The rustling leaves keep up a constant whispered commentary as you continue up the trail, while the hollow stalks knock against each other in the breeze with an eerie sound.

POOLS OF 'OHE'O

Haleakalā National Park

It has already come crashing over the Waimoku and the Makahiki Falls, but as it approaches the ocean the Palikea is still some 35 m (115 ft) above sea level. Hence its precipitous descent down 'Ohe'o Gulch, a deep and rocky – but thickly wooded – ravine through which it makes its way over a succession of cataracts and pools. It makes an in idyllic scene and it would be tempting to strip off and swim in these sunlit waters, but the banks positively bristle with notices warning the unwary of frequent rock falls.

ALIʻI KULA LAVENDER FARM

Upcountry Maui

A visit to this famous lavender farm is at once an education and an all-round sensory experience. It has become one of Maui's must-see attractions in recent years. Lying 1,220 m (4,000 ft) above sea level on the slopes of Haleakalā, Aliʻi Kula Lavender Farm pulls off the challenging feat of adding to the existing beauty of the island while further seducing with its smells. Lavender, we learn here, is not just one plant: 45 separate varieties are cultivated here, each one that little bit different from the last.

KULA BOTANICAL GARDENS

Upcountry Maui

They started out as a shop window for Warren and Helen McCord's landscaping business, but these extraordinary gardens have grown to be one of Maui's most popular attractions. Following Haleakalā's natural contours, over an area of 2.5 hectares (8 acres) the gardens incorporate a range of rock formations, streams and waterfalls, with additional artificial structures such as gazebos, a covered bridge and traditional tiki ancestor sculptures of the sort shown here. But pride of place is given to the plants: more than 2,000 different species, both indigenous and imported.

MAKAWAO

Upcountry Maui

Extensive grasslands in these lower foothills meant this area was ideal for ranching, making Makawao an improbable tropical take on the Wild West cow town in the nineteenth century. Hawaii's little-known native cowboys, the paniolos, congregated here, and its streets still have some of that slightly raffish air. Today it feels as far from Dodge City in tone as it is geographically. Its cafés and restaurants are highly regarded, while its stores offer an array of upmarket gifts for the discerning (and affluent) visitor, from fashions and fine art to jewellery and glass.

MAKAWAO RODEO

Upcountry Maui

A cowboy ropes a running cow at the Makawao Rodeo, an annual highlight here since the 1950s. Cowhand Harold 'Oskie' Rice, with several of his friends, felt it was important to celebrate the skills and cultural significance of the paniolo lifestyle that seemed to be coming under threat. Up to a point, the old ways have proven more resilient than might reasonably have been hoped: ranching certainly continues in the countryside. There is no doubt, however, that tourism has become the region's leading industry, to which the cowboys clearly have a contribution to make.

THE BIG ISLAND OF HAWAII – THE ORCHID ISLE

The island of Hawaii itself accounts for over 60 per cent of the archipelago's land area, but only 13 per cent of its population. Extensive areas of the island are all but empty. All the more room for orchids then. So, at least, you could be forgiven for thinking, given the island's climate and its popular nickname. In fact, of the 30,000 different orchid species, only three are indigenous to Hawaii and they are all very rare.

What is there here then? Only a fascinating history and the most wonderful range of natural scenery and wildlife. The many microclimates fostered by the steepness of the mountain slopes and the subtle differences dictated by aspect has meant a much more varied scene than might have been expected on an island of volcanic rock. No fewer than five separate volcanoes became fused together as flows of lava overlapped. The highest, Mauna Kea, reaches a height of 4,207 m (13,800 ft). Of the others, three remain active, meaning that this is an island still in the throes of formation, including some of the youngest rocks on Earth.

HILO

Hāmākua Coast

With only 43,000 inhabitants, the Big Island's principal urban centre scarcely qualifies as a city. However, it is an appealing place, with charming, quirky architecture to its name. A succession of tsunamis struck the town in the second half of the twentieth century, which are memorialized in the Pacific Tsunami Museum. Hilo has weathered more than its share of difficulties, including the collapse of the Hawaiian sugar industry in the 1990s and the eruption of Kīlauea in 2018, but remains a lively place. It is home to one of Hawaii's best farmers' markets, as well as numerous museums and other cultural attractions.

LILIʻUOKALANI PARK PARK AND GARDENS

Hāmākua Coast

Hawaii's last monarch, Queen Liliʻuokalani, left her most widely celebrated legacy in the song *Aloha 'Oe* (1878), but she also gave a grateful nation this plot of land. Liliʻuokalani died in 1893, however, and it was not until a quarter of a century later that it was laid out as an ornamental garden in the Japanese style. Even so, it was named in her honour, its sophisticated elegance and natural beauty a fitting tribute to a queen who had dedicated her reign to the promotion of Hawaiian life and culture.

HAWAII TROPICAL BOTANICAL GARDEN

Hāmākua Coast

An exquisite little glade slopes down the densely forested hillside above Onomea Bay. A little stream makes its headlong descent here, tumbling over several waterfalls. Since the 1970s, this lovely valley has been developed as a botanical garden, showcasing the natural flora of the Hawaiian forest; it was opened to the public in 1984. The founders' vision was more to curate the natural scene than to create an artificial, ornamental garden, and no fewer than 2,000 different plant species are represented here.

WAILUKU RIVER STATE PARK (RAINBOW FALLS)

Hāmākua Coast

At Hilo's north-western edge – just a short walk from the centre of the city – the urban area ends abruptly. A lovely state park has been established on the Wailuku's wooded banks. And here we see its centrepiece, where the river reaches a rock-shelf and rushes over, plunging 24 m (80 ft). An already impressive sight is made the more arresting at mid-morning, for it is then that the sun's rays catch the flying spray. The result is a breathtaking rainbow show – hence their Hawaiian name, Waianuenue, 'Rainbow Falls'.

ONOMEA BAY

Hāmākua Coast

The drive along the Hāmākua Coast to the north of Hilo is exhilarating; even by Hawaiian standards, the views to be had here are breathtaking. A definite highlight is the sight of Onomea Bay, accessible via the Old Mamalahoa Highway beyond Papaikou. Glimpsed from the road in passing, it is a scene of picture-postcard perfection; if you park up and take a stroll along one of several nearby woodland trails, however, approaching the blue waters through the ancient trees is a positively paradisiacal experience.

UMAUMA FALLS

Hāmākua Coast

Just downstream from the Hawaii Tropical Botanical Garden, a spectacular staircase of cataracts – three main falls – carries the waters through a descent of 91 m (300 ft). And all in the most magical of settings. The rocky gorge down which the stream cascades is a cornucopia of colourful vegetation – bright vermilions, softer russets, and reds and greens of every shade. If the aesthetic excitement is not enough to get the blood pumping, you can experience it all from a 3.2-km (2-mile) zipline, taking in breathtaking waterfall, forest and ocean views.

'AKAKA FALLS

Hāmākua Coast

Hawaii's landscapes were created in the utmost violence, its bedrocks bent, folded, twisted and tortured by immense geological forces over millions of years. But the result (at lower altitudes at least) is a scene of the utmost calm and peace. The 'Akaka Falls are a perfect example, the Kolekole Stream at this point plunging abruptly into an abyss 91 m (300 ft) deep. The kind of cataclysm needed to produce this faulting does not bear thinking about, yet the resultant scene is incredibly pleasing and benign.

LAUPĀHOEHOE POINT

Hāmākua Coast

In Hawaiian Laupāhoehoe simply means 'lava tip', an appropriate – if somewhat prosaic – name for this extraordinary headland. The sense of drama here is vague yet irresistible; these black basalt columns standing heroically firm but faintly quixotic too before the battering onslaught of the ocean waves. Hawaii's whole story, geographically, has been one of ceaseless struggle between fresh, volcanically created rock and the eternal erosion of the sea. So far, the islands have prevailed, producing rock that little bit faster than the ocean can destroy it – but the cost is registered in this coastline's ragged forms.

KAHŪNĀ FALLS

Hāmākua Coast

A little way downstream in the 'Akaka State Park the Kolekole flows over another cataract, the Kahūnā Falls. Though similar in height to the nearby 'Akaka Falls, at approximately 90 m (300 ft), it is always been seen as something of a 'poor relation'. Largely, though, this would seem to be because it is comparatively inaccessible; few sightseers get to see it close up in all its glory. Even as a distant prospect, though, it is a majestic sight by any standards, adding to the sublimity of the Hawaiian scene.

WAIPI'O VALLEY AND LOOKOUT

Hāmākua Coast

A breathtaking, if not heartstopping, vista. The USA's steepest road (with gradients of anything up to 25 per cent) connects this vertiginous viewpoint with the scene we survey here. Looking down from a height of 609 m (2,000 ft), we see below us through the trees the place where a winding river reaches the sea across a black-sand beach. The valley's name, Waipi'o, means 'curving water' and relates not to the river but to the crescent-shaped bay into which it finally flows and on into the ocean.

HI'ILAWE FALLS

Hāmākua Coast

A little way inland along the ridge from the Lookout (*see* page 91), the Lālākea Stream plunges into the Waipi'o Valley. Hawaii's highest waterfall, it has a drop of 442 m (1,450 ft). The highest it may be, but it is not necessarily the most impressive. As dramatic as its setting is, the volume of its flow has been unreliable in recent years. This is believed to be the result of water being diverted into irrigation schemes upstream; only during the rainiest periods have the Hi'ilawe Falls been at their very best.

HONOKA'A

Hāmākua Coast

This little town grew up in the early decades of the twentieth century as a centre servicing what was one of the Big Island's most prosperous agricultural and ranching regions. Owners and workers alike needed somewhere not only to come to for supplies but also a place where they could let off steam at weekends. Opened in 1930 by the Tanimoto family, this 'People's Theatre' (spelled European-style for extra sophistication!) showed films not only in Japanese and English but also in Spanish, Portuguese and Filipino, reflecting the diversity of the local community at this time.

PELE

Puna

Here offerings are left on a shrine to Pele, the ancient fire-goddess last seen changing Molokini to stone (*see* page 56). She has long been associated with Puna and with Pāhoa in particular (*see* below). This is not surprising, given the succession of fresh lava flows making their slow and treacly way down from Kīlauea over the centuries, most recently since June 2014. Hawaii's ancient pagan beliefs can now for the most part be safely consigned to 'tradition', 'folklore' or 'heritage', but, with such frightening forces involved, can one be too careful?

LAVA TREES STATE MONUMENT

Puna

Many of Kīlauea's eruptions have been effusive rather than explosive, but the lava these produce can still cause considerable destruction and across very wide areas, threatening communities over 35 km (22 miles) away. Flows that came through this forest south of Pāhoa in 1790 caught up these trees, enveloping them at ground level while their upper reaches burned away, creating moulds around their stumps to grotesque effect. The continuing danger posed by lava flows was underlined in 2018, when the state park had to be closed for several months.

KALAPANA

Puna

This charred and sterile wasteground was once a town. In 1990, lava flows from Kīlauea engulfed the area, immolating much of the modern built-up area. Parts of Kalapana still stand, however, so it fared far better than the neighbouring settlements of Kaimū or Kaimū Bay, both of which were completely buried. Where the red-hot lava reached the ocean it of course cooled rapidly in hissing clouds of steam and hardened into solid stone. In these infernal conditions a whole new coastline came into being.

KAIMŪ

Puna

There is not much to show here for so many centuries of settlement. A once-thriving community lies buried 15 m (50 ft) beneath this coal-black coast. Flows from Kīlauea had begun encroaching on Kaimū and Kaimū Bay during the 1980s; both settlements were completely engulfed in 1990. Time moves on, however, and Hawaiians have through history had to learn to be adaptable. A new highway has been laid out across the lava, new houses are gradually being built and coconut palms planted in the rich volcanic soils.

KA LAE

Kau

The southernmost extremity of Hawaii – and, consequently, of the United States – 'South Point' is believed to have been where the first Polynesian settlers in Hawaii landed after their long voyage from Tahiti. The archaeological record here goes back to the fourth century AD. In modern times, its exposed position and open aspect has made it the ideal site for a windfarm. It has also – given the teeming shoals attracted by the swirling of ocean currents around this headland – become an important departure point for fishing boats.

PUNALU'U BEACH AND HONU

Kau

Hawaiian honu, or green sea turtles (*Chelonia mydas*), come ashore on this beautiful black-sand beach between Pahala and Na'alehu. This endangered species has found a safe haven here. The sand, of course, owes its colour to its origins as basaltic lava, which, having flowed down the hillside above, cools and fragments as it meets the water of the ocean. The attritional action of the sea over millions of years has done the rest, reducing what were once enormous boulders to fine sand.

PUʻU ʻŌʻŌ, KĪLAUEA

Hawaii Volcanoes National Park

A shield volcano (*see* page 56), Kīlauea extends itself over several square kilometres, and still more widely when you count its lava flows. Its eruptions and its effusions of lava have not come from any single point but have been dispersed across the entire area of the shield, through volcanic vents. The most dramatic-looking of these is surely this one. Very much the volcanic cone of popular imagination, Puʻu ʻŌʻō was in constant eruption from 1983 until April 2018. An 11-km (7-mile) Crater Rim Drive offers views of all Kīlauea's main peaks.

HALEMAʻUMAʻU CRATER, KĪLAUEA

Hawaii Volcanoes National Park

The nearest thing on Earth to a glimpse of hell, the glow of Halemaʻumaʻu lights up a lurid sky, its fiery colours melding with the reds and pinks of the setting sun. Whilst it has been quiet for long periods, this crater has erupted as recently as 2018. An explosive eruption in 1790 killed a third of King Keōua Kūʻahuʻula's army, which was out campaigning against the forces of Kamehameha I (*see* page 42). Their footprints, preserved in hot ash below the summit before it solidified, can still be seen.

MAUNA LOA

Hawaii Volcanoes National Park

Seen here across an ashen landscape, studded with smaller
volcanic vent cones, Mauna Loa may be the biggest volcano on
Earth. It is believed to have pushed its way out of the sea some
400,000 years ago (though it would have been pushing its way
up from the ocean bed for 300,000 years or so before that).
That it has not grown even higher than its present 4,169 m
(13,679 ft) is down to the fact that, with an estimated volume
of 75,000 cubic km (18,000 cubic miles), its sheer mass pushes
down the Earth's crust beneath it.

MAUNA KEA AND OBSERVATORIES

Hawaii Volcanoes National Park

The summit of Hawaii's highest mountain stands 4,207 m (13,803 ft) above sea level. More important, though, is its height above the clouds. This has made it the ideal site for astronomical observatories; an arid climate and a lack of light pollution also help. These advantages notwithstanding, the placing of telescopes here was controversial, provoking vociferous criticism from environmentalists. And there was still more impassioned opposition from Native Hawaiian groups, who felt that these developments trampled on their traditional belief that these summit areas were sacred to the gods.

THURSTON LAVA TUBE

Hawaii Volcanoes National Park

Lava cools when it is exposed to the air above, so the upper surface of a flow can start to solidify even as the liquid lava flows on below. Potentially, then, when the eruption stops, the molten matter can drain away completely leaving an empty space, or 'tube', running for some distance beneath a carapace of hardened stone. Named for Lorrin Thurston, a local journalist who campaigned for the establishment of the Hawaii Volcanoes National Park, the Thurston Lava Tube is big enough to walk through, a dramatic volcanic cavern in the ground.

PUʻUHONUA O HŌNAUNAU
NATIONAL HISTORICAL PARK

Kona

This Puʻuhonua was an ancient temple and a sanctuary; fugitives from the law who came here could rely on the protection of its priests. So sacred was their right to refuge that it trumped the most serious sentences. Criminals, blasphemers, military deserters, wrongdoers who under normal circumstances would have been executed without mercy or hesitation, had to be looked after if they entered here. The fierce-looking statues we see here had the role of spiritual sentries, guarding the sanctity of the site.

HULIHEʻE PALACE

Kona

In its day a vacation residence for Hawaii's royals, this mansion was built out of black basalt rock; a coat of stucco gave it a more sophisticated, 'European' air. Hawaiian royalty, to whose nineteenth-century lives Huliheʻe Palace is now a museum, had an ambivalent relationship with a modern age in which the kind of kinship-loyalties and ancestral values they represented were not understood – or, really, respected. The town of Kailua-Kona was for a time the kingdom's capital. Today it is an important commercial and tourist centre, and a living museum of Hawaiian culture.

AHUʻENA HEIAU

Kona

King Kamehameha I died here in 1819, his work of unifying
the Hawaiian isles complete. This heiau (the word simply
means 'temple') was the shrine in which he worshipped all his
gods. But it was a great deal more than this: it was a symbolic
tabernacle for his personal identity, his kingly authority and his
regal power; also a political headquarters in which he conferred
each night with his counsellors. Built atop a lava platform beside
Kailua Bay, it was a simple thatched construction, lovingly
restored in the 1990s.

MANTA RAYS AND SNORKELLING

Kona

The seas around Hawaii are not exactly short of exciting diving spots, but the Kona coast has a special status for sub-aqua fans. Snorkellers in particular love the stretch just to the south of Kailua-Kona. It is a divers' paradise with its crystalline waters, companionable dolphins, an extraordinary range of exotic fish and stupendous reefs. For real aficionados, though, the ultimate experience is a nocturnal dive in a quest for that most magnificent, and enigmatic, of ocean creatures – the manta ray.

HOLUALOA COUNTRY AND COFFEE

Kona

Kona coffee is world-famous and indeed it is exported to every corner of the globe, but locals are determined not to miss out. In Holualoa, at the heart of the coffee-growing region, the beverage has acquired a quasi-patriotic significance: they do not just fly the flag, they drink the drink. Not that they neglect the other aspects of café culture, its association with the creative and sophisticated life. Holualoa has almost as many art galleries as it does coffee shops.

KALOKO-HONOKŌHAU NATIONAL HISTORICAL PARK

Kona

King Kamehameha I had this temple built to Kūkaʻilimoku, god of war, in 1790. At the time, Kamehameha was locked in a frustrating stalemate with his cousin and bitter rival Keōua Kūʻahuʻula. The construction was the least of the labour involved; every block was brought by human chain from the Valley of Pololū, 22 km (14 miles) to the east. It may have been that Kūkaʻilimoku was moved by Kamehameha's efforts to appease him: Keōua Kūʻahuʻula ran into trouble (*see* page 101) and Kamehameha was able to claim his victory.

PUʻUKOHOLĀ HEIAU NATIONAL HISTORIC SITE

Kohala

The site seems bleak – the outer edge of a black and barren lava flow. Agriculture must have been just about unthinkable down here. Still, something must have drawn the first Hawaiian settlers so many centuries ago. There may have been religious ties to a place where the forces of fire and water met, but there would have been other attractions. To this day, turtles come ashore to lay their eggs; there are hand-built fishponds dating back 300 years; and there would have been an abundance of shellfish and seabirds' eggs as well.

PUAKO PETROGLYPH ARCHEOLOGICAL PRESERVE

Kohala

Hawaii's earliest inhabitants did not read or write, but they expressed themselves almost compulsively in petroglyphs (literally 'rock carvings'): there are more than 3,000 at Puako alone. We cannot hope to fathom their message: archaeologists acknowledge their ignorance of what the meaning or function of these carvings was, beyond a suspicion that they may have recorded individuals' births and deaths and important community events. There is no doubt, though, that they seem to speak to us across the barriers of time and culture. That is what makes a visit to Puako so memorable and so moving.

WAIMEA

Kohala

Also known as Kamuela, in part to differentiate it from the Waimea in Kauai (*see* pages 30–33), this Waimea lies in the foothills of Kohala, a region of open grassland famous for its ranches and cowboy culture. These rolling plains and the paniolo lifestyle are perhaps un-Hawaiian in stereotypical terms and yet, as we have seen, they are encountered on other islands (*see* page 77). A rodeo is held in Waimea each year and there is even a museum dedicated to the history and the culture of the paniolo (the Paniolo Heritage Center).

KOHALA MOUNTAIN ROAD

Kohala

The locals call it the 'High Road', and they are not wrong.
Route 250 follows a north–south line around the western slopes
of Kohala, the oldest of Hawaii's five main volcanoes. Starting
west of Waimea in the south, it ends at Hāwī, on Hawaii's
northern coast. Though it never scales the mountain heights,
it climbs to altitudes of 1,006 m (3,500 ft) in its central sections
and – as can easily be imagined – offers some stunning views.
And these are not just of Kohala; here we look across to the
distant form of Mauna Kea.

HĀWĪ

Kohala

Triathletes know this pretty little town from the part it plays
in the annual Ironman World Championship. Hāwī is the
turning point in the cycle leg. It is only 159 m (522 ft) above
sea level, but the climb up the Kona coast road from Kawaihae
is lung-busting – though the return journey is of course
correspondingly a breeze! Those who prefer to see
their triathlons on TV from the comfort of their sofas will
find plenty to engage them in Hāwī's quirky cafés, restaurants,
shops and galleries.

KAMEHAMEHA STATUE

Kohala

Kapaʻau's claim to fame is as the birthplace of King Kamehameha I, who unified the Hawaiian islands in the nineteenth century. His statue has had almost as adventurous a life as its subject did: commissioned in the 1870s, it was cast in Paris and then sent by sea. The ship that was carrying it was unfortunately wrecked off the Falkland Islands. The Hawaiians went ahead and had a replacement made, but subsequently the Falklanders found the original and it was brought here to take its rightful place.

LAPAKAHI STATE HISTORICAL PARK

Kohala

This old Hawaiian fishing village in its ravishingly beautiful setting is believed to date back at least 600 years. The ruins extend across an area of 1,040 hectares (2,560 acres). They include not only heiau (temples) but also smaller shrines and sacred objects, as well as a large burial site where bodies were interred over generations. Then there are the more prosaic, secular, remains: houses, rock shelters, a saltpan, a well, walled pens, a roofed barn for storing canoes – even a rubbish dump full of discarded seashells.

O'AHU – THE GATHERING PLACE

Two volcanoes joined together to make up what is now Hawaii's third-largest island: Wai'anae in the west and Ko'olau in the east. The lava flows that linked them form a sort of central plain. Honolulu, Hawaii's largest city and the capital of the US state, is situated on the island's southern coast. O'ahu's population – pushing one million, some two-thirds of Hawaii's total – is swollen by the stream of tourists year round.

An estimated five million visitors come each year to enjoy the unlimited sun, sea and sand, not to mention nightlife. Or, for the more intrepid, outdoor sports from scuba diving and sailing to rock climbing and caving. For lovers of natural and human history, there is hiking and fascinating flora and fauna to observe. There is a range of intriguing archaeological sites to visit, not only ancient Hawaiian settlements but much more recent remains, like the memorialized wrecks of the US ships sunk in the Japanese attack on Pearl Harbor in 1941. In short, O'ahu has something for everyone. Most of all, though, O'ahu has itself: its mountain slopes are sublimely beautiful; its rocky gorges and waterfalls spectacular; and its woods and forests just take the breath away.

HONOLULU

Honolulu

A modern city in a timeless jewel of a setting in the shadow of
a mountain on the shores of an azure sea. All this and a balmy
tropical climate. Hawaii's capital could hardly be more blessed in
terms of its location. Though already occupied for centuries by
the Hawaiians, Honolulu was 'discovered' by Britain's 'Butterworth
Squadron' commanded by Captain William Brown in 1794. It grew
rapidly in importance, not just as an entry point for the Hawaiian
islands but also as a mid-Pacific staging post for shipping between
North America and Asia.

WAIKIKI

Honolulu

This famous Honolulu neighbourhood has at times been
a victim of its own success. So many hotels had been built
here by the mid-twentieth century and so close were they
crowding to the shore that the physical integrity of the beach
was being threatened. In the decades that followed, it had to be
reconstructed almost in its entirety using imported sand, so what
we see now is an elaborate pretence. It does the trick, though:
Waikiki beach is as delightful a playground as it ever was.

LEONARD'S BAKERY

Honolulu

Leonard's Bakery on Kapahulu Avenue is home to the world-famous malasada, essentially a sweet and tender deep-fried doughnut. Like Leonard's original founder, Frank Leonard Rego, who began his business here in 1952, this delicacy was of Portuguese origin. In the old country, it occupied the same sort of culinary niche as the Shrove Tuesday pancake does in other countries – a way of using up eggs and fat on the eve of Lent for Mardi Gras. Though Leonard's has now expanded significantly from its original bakery, it remains a family business to this day.

CHINATOWN

Honolulu

Asian Americans account for a good half of Honolulu's population. Almost 20 per cent are of Japanese origin and 10 per cent Chinese. For the most part the descendants of indentured labourers brought in to work O'ahu's plantations in the nineteenth century, these groups have been here for quite some time. There are also Koreans, Laotians, Thais and Vietnamese. This cultural diversity is reflected most obviously here in the city's architecture, but also in everything from art and music to restaurant cuisine.

DIAMOND HEAD STATE MONUMENT (LEʻAHI)

Honolulu

This volcanic peak overlooking Honolulu is technically a western offshoot of the Koʻolau system (*see* page 159), one of a great many vents and cones associated with that great shield volcano. For the people of Honolulu, however, it is very much its own mountain, as emblematic for them as Mount Fuji is for Tokyo or Table Mountain for Cape Town. It takes its name, it is said, from the glistening calcite crystals to be found on nearby beaches – mistaken by impressionable British sailors for real diamonds.

NATIONAL MEMORIAL CEMETERY OF THE PACIFIC

Honolulu

Tens of thousands of US servicemen and servicewomen were killed in the course of the Second World War; many fell in far-flung places across a vast Pacific theatre. It made sense, when the war ended, to have those bodies that could be found brought to a central place where they could be interred together, somewhere their families and former comrades – and their grateful fellow citizens – could readily come to thereafter to pay their respects. Over 50,000 were laid to rest here, including US veterans of other wars.

SHANGRI LA

Honolulu

The wealthy tobacco heiress Doris Duke built this palatial residence on the slopes of Diamond Head in the 1930s. A socialite and surfer (long before the sport was fashionable with non-Hawaiians), Duke had a scandalous private life. But she also had a much more serious side. No one did more than she to campaign for the preservation of historical architecture in America. She was also a horticulturalist of note and a major collector of Islamic art. Her collection can be viewed at her Honolulu home, which has now become a world-famous museum.

DUKE KAHANOMOKU STATUE

Honolulu

'Duke' was his first name, not a title, but this son of Honolulu was a man of immense distinction. He thoroughly deserves both this bronze statue and the leis he has been bedecked with here. Of Native Hawaiian origin, Kahanomoku, who was born a few blocks away from this site on the Waikiki shore, grew up to promote the message of Hawaiian beach-culture worldwide. He did this not just as an Olympic swimmer but as the first real popularizer of the sport of surfing, and as a movie actor and businessman.

ALOHA TOWER

Honolulu

The one Hawaiian word that just about everyone knows, 'aloha' betokens both loving friendship and warmth of welcome. It makes sense, then, for it to have been bestowed as a title on the great lighthouse that greeted vessels approaching Honolulu's harbour. Standing 56 m (120 ft) tall, its tower is visible for many miles across the ocean. Its construction was completed in 1926. Like the harbour district as a whole, the Aloha Tower now has a neglected air. The hope is that plans to redevelop the area will work out.

KAWAIAHA'O CHURCH

Honolulu

'Hawaii's Westminster Abbey' was built in 1820 – one of the oldest places of Christian worship in the state. A Congregational church, it was constructed entirely out of coral blocks, so marries local materials with European style. Before the (Episcopalian) Cathedral Church of Saint Andrew was built at the end of the 1860s, Kawaiaha'o did service as the kingdom's national church, with the royal family coming to worship here. Rows of royal portraits are displayed above the sanctuary, a colourful reminder of an age gone by.

'IOLANI PALACE

Honolulu

Kamehameha III (1814–54) had this impressive royal residence built, though it was not completed until 25 years after his death. The second son of Kamehameha I, he had inherited the Hawaiian crown from his elder brother in 1825. A thoughtful man and a modernizer, he oversaw the monarchy's transition from absolutism to constitutionality. Successive rulers would live here until the reign of Lili'uokalani (*see* page 80), at which time, in 1893, the monarchy was overthrown.

BISHOP MUSEUM

Honolulu

Hawaii's main museum is a treasure house of Polynesian and Pacific life and culture, crammed with all manner of important artefacts plus a comprehensive collection of flora and fauna from the region. Hawaiian Princess Bernice Pauhi Bishop co-founded the museum in 1889 with her husband, the US banker Charles Reed Bishop. The original collection was constructed around the Princess's Hawaiian heirlooms; she was after all a member of the ruling royal house. It grew rapidly, though, and came to be one of the world's great museums.

KOKO HEAD CRATER TRAIL

Honolulu

Once a working funicular railway transported supplies up the side of this volcanic headland, to the US military lookout post placed just below its crater. Now only its tracks remain to tease those toiling on foot. Still, the chance to peer into the crater and to look out and see the panoramic views extending in every direction will surely make those efforts all worthwhile.

HANAUMA BAY NATURE PRESERVE

Honolulu

This bay at O'ahu's south-east corner is actually a drowned volcanic crater. And quite clearly visibly so, when viewed from above. For the holidaymakers and day-trippers, it is one of the most dazzling snorkelling spots for miles around, where beach-goers can simply wade into a coral reef teeming with tropical fish. In recent years their needs have had to be balanced with those of the bay's breeding green turtles and other sea life: currently the beach is closed to visitors on Tuesdays, to give the wildlife a weekly break.

PEARL HARBOR

Central O'ahu

On the morning of Sunday, 7 December 1941, the USS *Arizona* went down here with all 1,177 hands – just one of eight warships sunk in a surprise air-attack by the Japanese. The other vessels were subsequently salvaged, but the Arizona was beyond repair and, so many souls being lost, it seemed fitting to preserve it as a war grave. Hence this floating shrine, a memorial to all the 2,403 military personnel and civilians who lost their lives in the attack. Hundreds of thousands of visitors pay their respects each year.

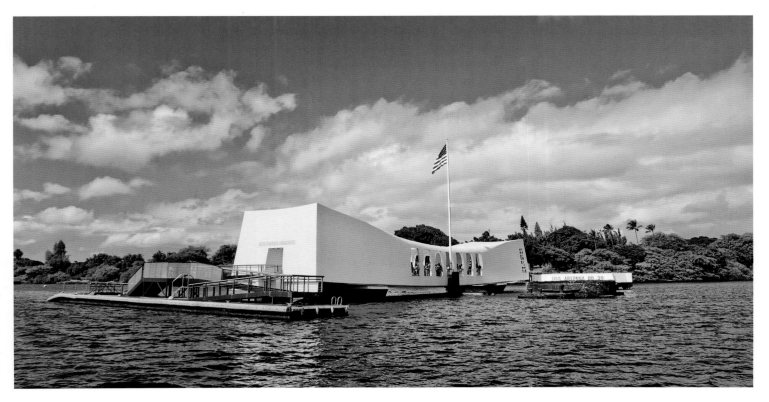

WAI'ANAE MOUNTAINS

Central O'ahu

Their sheer walls corrugated by water run-off, the austere
line of the Wai'anae Mountains makes a stark, strong contrast
with the greenery and freshness of Ma'akua Gulch. Whilst it
is conventionally characterized as a mountain range, Wai'anae
is really one continuous ridge – the eroded massif of a single
shield volcano – that makes up much of O'ahu's western side.
The valleys in this district are deep and fertile, but for the most
part undeveloped, making them the ideal habitat for a wondrous
variety of wildlife species.

DOLE PINEAPPLES, WAHIAWA

Central Oʻahu

The low and level lands of Oʻahu's central valley have been seen as prime plantation territory for a century or so. Water brought down from the hills for use in irrigation is stored in an artificial reservoir, Lake Wilson. Dole pineapples are perhaps the region's best-known product: the company has been based here since 1901, though it can arguably trace its operational lineage back as far as the 1850s. With revenues of some $4.5 billion and well over 30,000 employees, it makes a considerable contribution to Oʻahu's economic life.

HAWAII PLANTATION VILLAGE

Central Oʻahu

The plantation system brings to agriculture the mass-production methods of modern industry. The work is labour-intensive but unskilled. Although the sort of chattel slavery seen in the Deep South was passing into history by the time Hawaii's plantations were coming into production, that does not mean that they were not oppressive in their way. The indentured workers recruited locally among the Hawaiians and shipped in from Japan, China and so many other countries had to pay off their passage, food and accommodation – at rates determined by the companies – before they could hope to see a cent in pay.

MĀKAHA BEACH PARK

Leeward Coast

White surf in bright blue water seems to reflect the fluffy clouds of a clear blue sky in this mesmeric scene. The sandy beach stands out between them like a gash of gold. Mākaha, north-west of Wai'anae, is a favourite spot for winter surfing, and a watersports centre all year round – a great place for diving, kayaking and body boarding. It is also a haven for wildlife, the beach a nesting place for several turtle species and the offshore coral reefs home to a wide variety of fish.

YOKOHAMA OR KEAWAULA BAY

Leeward Coast

Popularly known as Yokohama in honour of the famous Japanese seaport, Keawaula Bay has the northernmost sandy beach on O'ahu's western coast. It is correspondingly quiet for the most part, though there are generally surfers and swimmers about, cavorting in the waves under the watchful gaze of the lifeguard. Conditions can be treacherous, the winter waves especially big and violent, frequently rising up to 15 m (49 ft) and sometimes, according to anecdote, a great deal higher. Close up against Ka'ena Point, there is a savage undertow. Yokohama must be treated with respect.

KA'ENA POINT

Leeward Coast

Strike inland from Yokohama and you find the Ka'ena Trail, winding uphill through thorny thickets and scrub. It is vital not to leave the path, for rare seabirds (including albatrosses and shearwaters) nest here at ground level. The trail eventually takes you to the top of Ka'ena Point, Oa'hu's westernmost extremity. In ancient folklore departing souls stepped off Ka'ena to follow the setting sun. The ocean views here are extraordinarily striking. Seabirds soar and wheel above, while endangered monk seals gather on the rocks below. This is nature at its most unspoiled and sublime.

WAIMEA BAY

North Shore

Another island, another Waimea (*see* pages 30–33 and 114).
The Hawaiian name seems simply to mean 'reddish water' –
frequently found given the archipelago's volcanic soils. Across the
water we see the white tower of the (Catholic) Mission of Saints
Peter and Paul, but Waimea Bay boasts a pagan place of worship
too. The ruins of an ancient temple, Puʻu o Mahuka Heiau, stand
on the hillside above the beach. Its Hawaiian name means 'Hill
of Escape', supposedly in reference to the fire goddess Pele's leap
from here to the next island.

HALE'IWA

North Shore

More than half a century has passed since the surf boom started in the Sixties. The ultimate youth pursuit has come of age – and then some. Not that it makes too much sense to see it as simply a sport, a pastime. Surfing is a way of life, with its own subculture, its own fashions, its own slang. Surfers are deeply serious about their fun, fun, fun…. Nowhere is this Peter Pan character more clearly visible than it is in Hale'iwa, the acknowledged capital of North Shore surfing.

BANZAI PIPELINE AND SURFING

North Shore

Huge waves break over a flat-topped but sharp-edged coral reef, creating a tube-like space through which the skilled surfer can ride. There is no more notorious reef-break in the world than the Banzai Pipeline. Surfers gather here from all over the world – you might almost call them pilgrims, such is their dedication to their sport and their reverence for these rollers – to try their skills, strength and courage against the most monstrous waves, not just here but all along O'ahu's North Shore.

SHAVED ICE

North Shore

This Hawaiian treat is just what it sounds like: fine ice shavings taken from a frozen core and flavoured with a range of local tastes, from guava or lychee to coconut, pineapple or passion fruit. The basic concept seems to have been brought to the islands by Japanese immigrants in the nineteenth century but it has now 'gone native' in its adoptive home. And, in the process, it has acquired some US touches, frequently being served with a dollop of ice cream in a fast-food plastic cup.

MAKAPU'U POINT

Windward Coast

This dramatic rock-bound promontory marks O'ahu's easternmost extremity. It represented a real hazard to shipping for many years. The lighthouse here, built in 1909, is officially a historic monument now – though it is also a working light, in active use. A little way along the coast, at the summit of the headland on its northern side, is a lookout offering stunning ocean views. Below in the bay to the northwest is the Makapu'u Beach – said to be the finest beach for body boarding in all Hawaii.

NU'UANU PALI LOOKOUT

Windward Coast

Ko'olau's rocky massif falls away abruptly in a pali (or 'cliff') at the head of the Nu'uanu Valley. Since the 1960s road tunnels have run directly through the mountain here to Honolulu, Hawaii's great metropolis now no more than a short drive away. On this side of the shield, though, the Nu'uanu Pali Lookout gives out on to open space, green trees, blue skies, scudding clouds and blessed peace, with uninterrupted views across country all the way down to the coastal township of Kāne'ohe.

KAILUA AND LANIKAI

Windward Coast

A quiet and comfortable residential town, Kailua has sometimes struggled to come to terms with the number of tourists drawn here – especially since US President Barack Obama set up his 'Winter White House' here. If its beach is well worth the trip from Honolulu, the more southerly strand at Lanikai is in a different league: utterly, ecstatically, ravishing in its beauty. Even more than Kailua, this beach has been a victim of its own success: at weekends especially, it is difficult to find a free square inch of sand.

PILLBOX HIKE AND VIEW OVER KAILUA, LANIKAI AND ISLANDS

Windward Coast

High up on the bluff above Lanikai Beach stand a couple of wartime bunkers, their brutal concrete now a canvas for graffiti art. Though these pillboxes are not worth a pilgrimage themselves, the heights on which they stand most certainly are. The walk, though very steep, is also short, and the views – of Lanikai, Kailua and the ocean – are striking. Just a little way out to sea stand the Mokulua Islands – a pair of what were originally volcanic cones. Today they are important seabird sanctuaries.

KO'OLAU RANGE

Windward Coast

Like Wai'anae (*see* page 140) in the east, the more westerly of
O'ahu's two great volcanic massifs is often loosely regarded as
a mountain range. We view it here across the rippling waters of
the ancient Moli'i Fishpond, which occupies the northern end
of Kāne'ohe Bay. A 1,200-m (4,000-ft) wall of close-fitting stone
slabs and coral fragments was used to delimit the area in which
the fish were penned. Seawater could seep in but there was
not space between the stones for the fish to get out. A series of
sluices regulated the water flow.

HAIKU STAIRS

Windward Coast

Often also known as the 'Stairway to Heaven', this
celebrated trail takes the intrepid hiker straight up the side of
Pu'ukeahiakahoe. Standing at an altitude of 859 m (2,820 ft), this
summit – another offshoot of Ko'olau – commands outstanding
views across Kāne'ohe and its bay. It is literally a staircase: a
walkway with just shy of 4,000 steps was first installed here in
the 1940s. This was intended to facilitate access for workers
constructing a wireless signals system on behalf of the US Navy,
but was renewed in 2003 for the use of hikers.

BYODO-IN TEMPLE, VALLEY OF THE TEMPLES MEMORIAL PARK

Windward Coast

Though it is modelled on a 900-year-old original in Kyoto, this splendid shrine only dates back to 1968. That year marked the centenary of the first Japanese immigrants in Hawaii and the shrine was built in commemoration of that event. Their subsequent history has not been uniformly easy by any means. The earliest immigrants came as plantation labourers and anti-Asian prejudice continued for generations. It intensified in the aftermath of the Pearl Harbor attack and thousands of Japanese-Americans were interned during the Second World War, both in Hawaii and the continental USA.

LĀNA'I AND MOLOKA'I

There are hundreds of islands in the Hawaiian archipelago, though most of these are little more than rocks. Overwhelmingly – and understandably – tourists flock to the largest islands: Big Island, Kauai, Maui and O'ahu. Lāna'i and Moloka'i are often overlooked. By no means insignificant in size, Lāna'i extends over 364 square km (140 square miles). Its volcanic peak, Lana'ihale, rises to 1,026 m (3,330 ft). Its population is tiny, though, standing at a little over 3,000. It is thought to have been among the last of the main islands to be occupied when the Polynesians first came.

Moloka'i is almost twice the size, covering an area of 670 square km (260 square miles); it has double the population too – over 7,300 souls. Like O'ahu, it came into being when two adjacent shield volcanoes (in this case East Moloka'i and West Moloka'i) were fused together, their lava flows forming a connecting central plain. In addition to their different aspects, the size disparity between the two peaks – West Moloka'i is much smaller and much lower – has produced a divergence in ecological conditions across the island. In the east it is lush, fresh and forested, whereas in the west it is arid, even semi-desert in places.

LĀNAʻI CITY

Central Lānaʻi

Lānaʻi has long been known as 'Pineapple Island'. Between the 1920s and the 1990s, the Dole company ran the world's biggest pineapple plantation here. Sugar too was produced in Lānaʻi, but it too has since declined, and in recent decades the emphasis has been on tourism. It has not been easy: visitors' vacation time is all too short, of course, and there is so much to see and do on Hawaii's larger islands. Lānaʻi remains something of a niche interest; gradually, though, interest has been growing.

MUNRO TRAIL

Central Lānaʻi

This rugged route, to be attempted only by the determined off-road driver or the hardy hiker, leads from Lānaʻi City all the way up the side of Lanaʻihale. Overall, that is a distance of some 20 km (13 miles). The views from its summit are awe-inspiring. In clear conditions you can see all the way across to the Big Island with its two highest mountains, Mauna Loa and Mauna Kea, as well as Kauai, Maui and Oʻahu. But there are ravishing vistas to be seen from many other points along the way.

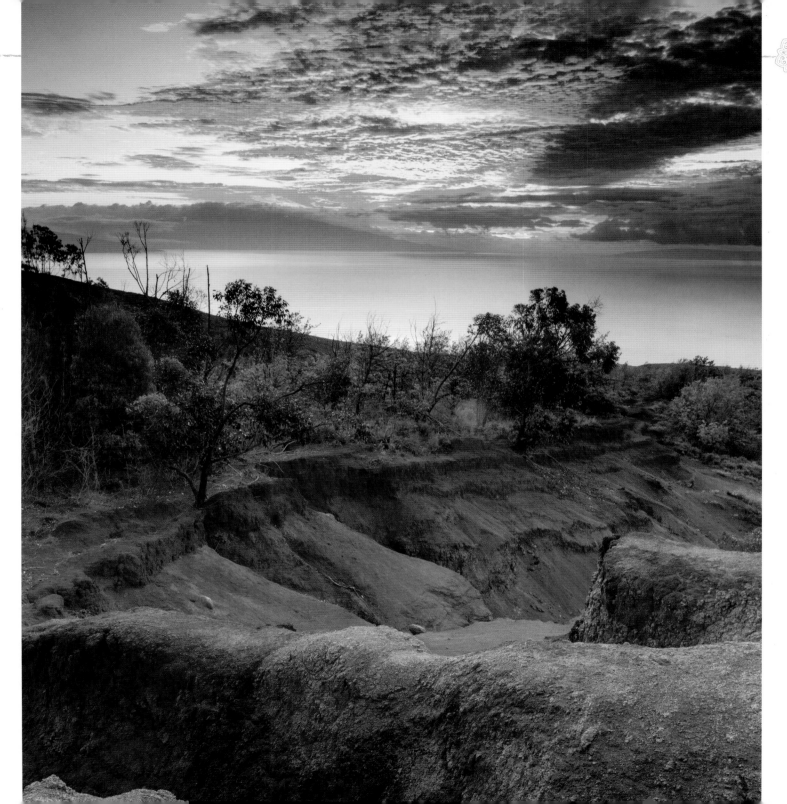

KAIOLOHIA OR SHIPWRECK BEACH

North Lāna'i

A dramatic setting, an evocative name, but the story behind it could hardly be less romantic. Dismiss ideas of old four-masters or buccaneers. The stricken hulk that lies offshore here was one of a number of ferroconcrete barges built by the US in their haste to build up their haulage capacities in the Pacific War. Perhaps no historical detail should be beneath our notice. However, surely this is a shipwreck that only a Second World War fanatic or an engineering geek could love. Nevertheless, this point of interest enhances an already striking vista.

KEAHIAKAWELO OR GARDEN OF THE GODS

North Lāna'i

This martian landscape lies near the northwestern tip of Lāna'i. How is this scene of utter sterility to be explained? The ancient Hawaiians attempted it by saying that two kahunas or priests – one here and one on Moloka'i – vied with one another over who could keep a fire going for longest. Lāna'i's man won, but only by stripping this part of his island of every blade of grass, every leaf and every twig. Modern scientists point, prosaically, to the effects of erosion on an area in the 'rain shadow' cast by hills rising to the east.

HULOPOE BEACH

South Lānaʻi

With its swaying palms, its crescent of white coral sand and its bright blue lapping waves, Lānaʻi's favourite beach is as close an approximation to the tropical island ideal as you will find. It is certainly a match for any in Hawaii, as the holidaymakers who come here each year to sunbathe, swim and snorkel will attest. This being Lānaʻi, though, the numbers coming are limited compared to those thronging the more famous beaches on the Big Island or Oʻahu. It never feels uncomfortably crowded here.

PUʻU PEHE

South Lānaʻi

A young man named Makakehau and a maiden, Pehe, fell in love, it is said, and would sit for hours together on these rocks. They would sleep together in a cave beneath the cliffs nearby. One day, however, Makakehau saw his beloved swept away by a storm-surge. Though he plunged into the waves to save her, she was drowned. He buried her body on top of this towering (24-m/80-ft) stack and then, despairing, leapt off it to his death.

KAUNOLŪ VILLAGE SITE

South Lāna'i

Kamehameha I spent lengthy holidays here, partly to get
away from the hubbub and the stress of court life but partly
(presumably) to get closer to his cultural roots. This historic
village was only abandoned in the 1880s but appears to
have been settled for several centuries by then. Not far from
Kamehameha's residence is a ruined temple, Halulu Heiau.
From a cleft in the cliff top nearby, named Kahekili's Leap
after a famous warrior of the eighteenth century, young men
showed their courage by hurling themselves into the ocean
24 m (80 ft) below.

SHARK FIN COVE

South Lāna'i

The fearsome-looking shark fin on the far horizon is fortunately
just a jagged rock formation. Good news, given the importance
of this cove at Kaunolū as a diving and snorkelling site. The sea
here, above a gorgeous coral reef, is exceptionally rich in fish,
hence the establishment of Kaunolū in the first place and the
time Kamehameha, a keen fisherman, spent here. But other
exotic sea creatures are also to be seen, from manta rays to
spinner dolphins – even whale sharks.

KALAUPAPA PENINSULA

Central Moloka'i

To us this seems too beautiful to be a place of banishment, but generations of Hawaiians learned to think of it with dread. This rocky peninsula juts out from Moloka'i's northern coast, an isolated outcrop of an already isolated island. Hence the decision to turn the place into a leper colony. The modern orthodoxy is that leprosy (or Hansen's Disease) is not especially infectious; it is the damage and disfigurement it produces in the sufferer's face and limbs that has led the disease to be regarded with such horror. Even so, the Kalaupapa colony was not closed down until 1969. The Kalaupapa National Historical Park was created to preserve the settings of Moloka'i's leper colonies at Kalaupapa and Kalawao for posterity, and to foster public understanding of the disease.

FATHER DAMIEN

Central Moloka'i

Belgian by birth, Saint Damien of Moloka'i (1840–89) went to Hawaii in 1864 to work as a missionary. He was ordained as a priest on his arrival in Honolulu. When the need arose for chaplains for the new settlement at Kalaupapa, Damien was the first to volunteer. He worked there, ministering to the lepers from 1873, heedless of the risk to his own health. In fact, he seems to have been fine for 11 years. Famously, he realized he had contracted the disease when he doused his feet with boiling water, but felt no pain.

ANCIENT HAWAIIAN FISHPONDS

Central Moloka'i

Aquaculture is a Hawaiian thing. We have seen – at Alekoko, Kauai (*see* page 27), Kaloko-Honokōhau (*see* page 113) and Moli'i (*see* page 159) – fishponds allowing the partial cultivation of the sea. Something broadly similar was seen in the 'fish traps' of medieval Europe, but there was no precedent in Polynesian tradition. Believed to date back 700 years, the ponds on Moloka'i are particularly fine. The opening in the foreground would have been blocked by a wooden gate. Fish swimming in would stay for the algae cultivated there and, growing fat, be unable to find their way out again.

KAPUAIWA COCONUT GROVE

Central Moloka'i

This is no ordinary coconut grove. Standing outside Kaunakakai, on Moloka'i's southern coast, it was planted in the 1860s by King Kamehameha V, who had a summer residence near here. Though only a few hundred palms survive, there were originally a thousand, the resulting forest extending over 4 hectares (10 acres). Each tree represented a warrior in his army. Kamehameha V, wrote Mark Twain, who visited his court in 1866, was 'a wise sovereign … popular, greatly respected, and even beloved'.

KANEMITSU'S BAKERY, KAUNAKAKAI

Central Moloka'i

By day it is an unassuming bakery-cum-coffee shop, though its bread and pastries are uniformly praised and it is the perfect place for breakfast or lunch. Come evening, however, the café closes and Kanemitsu's throws off this modest, daytime guise. Late-night visitors queue in the alley behind to buy its sensational 'hot bread', straight from the oven. Soft and doughy, it is sold crammed with fillings from blackberry or strawberry jam to cream cheese, cinnamon or sugar. 'A feast', according to *The New York Times*.

POST-A-NUT, HO'OLEHUA POST OFFICE

Central Moloka'i

Walking in the Kapuaiwa Coconut Grove (*see* page 174) is not recommended. The unwary can be badly hurt by falling fruit. Souvenir seekers can, however, avail themselves of a handy 'Post-a-Nut' service run by the Post Office in Ho'olehua, a few kilometres away. A big part of the fun is decorating the nuts in bright colours and bold designs prior to posting. They provide the nuts and colouring materials; you just have to pay the postage. The perfect gift for friends and relatives back home.

MAUNALOA AND BIG WIND KITE FACTORY

West End

Not to be confused with the Big Island's big mountain, Mauna Loa (*see* page 102), Moloka'i's Maunaloa is a little township near the island's western shore. Once this was a thriving market centre serving the nearby plantations, but things have quietened down considerably since they closed. Now it is chiefly famous as the home of Big Wind Kites. Since 1980, Daphne and Jonathan Socher have been selling brightly coloured 'creative kites' and windsocks (personally customized if required), as well as more general decorations and gifts.

PAPOHAKU OR THREE-MILE BEACH

West End

Though one of the longest and most achingly beautiful coral–sand beaches in the Hawaiian islands, Papohaku is also one of the most impossibly secluded. Way out on Moloka'i's western coast, it is far enough from Kaunakakai to make getting here a major undertaking. But while it is a designated beach park, you could never call it a resort. There is a campsite here, with basic conveniences, but no shops, cafés or other amenities, so the three miles of sand and surf are about it.

KAMAKOU PRESERVE

East End

Moloka'i's bigger, eastern volcanic massif has its highest peak in Kamakou, which reaches an altitude of 1,512 m (4,961 ft). Its upper slopes are cloaked in forest, home to 250 rare plant species, the vast majority unknown outside Hawaii. Endangered birds are to be seen as well. The 1,095-hectare (2,700-acre) preserve is carefully protected by Nature Conservancy staff; access is limited to monthly tours, and walkers have to follow wooden boardwalks. Even so, the overwhelming impression the visitor gets is of unmanaged wilderness – an untouched, indeed positively primeval, place.

HĀLAWA VALLEY AND HĪPUAPUA FALLS

East End

The Hālawa Valley is believed to have been the first bit of Moloka'i to be settled by the Polynesian adventurers who arrived here in the seventh century. The record they and their successors have left behind in their rock art is beautiful, if bemusing. Sadly, having survived so long, their settlements were largely washed away by a tsunami in 1946. Today's visitors mostly come to see the waterfalls. The Hīpuapua Falls are 152 m (500 ft) in height, though access is so difficult they are really only visible from the air.

MOAʻULA FALLS

East End

Downstream from the Hīpuapua Falls (*see* page 180), the Moaʻula Falls at about 75 m (250 ft), are much less high, but they are more spectacularly framed as the waters roar down a rocky outcrop in a densely wooded forest glade. They are also vastly more accessible. The visitor even gets to round off the 7-km (4.5-mile) hike with a swim in the deep plunge pool at the foot of the cataract. Again, the walk here is through country that was for centuries home to a thriving community, passing petroglyphs, ruined stone walls and an old heiau shrine.

KUMIMI BEACH

East End

This lovely stretch of shoreline is more popularly known as Murphy's Beach — or, indeed, Twenty-Mile Beach. Not because it is anything like that long (it does not actually account for much more than half a kilometre of coast) but because it stands at the 20-mile marker on Molokaʻi's main Kamehameha V Highway. It is a superb spot for snorkelling, since its waters are so crystal clear when calm, though when the wind is stronger the surf gets up here in no uncertain terms.

HALAWA BAY

East End

The first Polynesian arrivals in Moloka'i seem to have landed
here 1,300 years ago before establishing their settlements up
the valley (*see* page 180). Which beach they came ashore on, we
have no way of knowing, for there are two, situated side by side,
thanks to the peculiar formation of the bay. The visitor gets to
choose between Kama'alaea, to the west, and Kawili, to the east.
Both are equally beautiful, though Kama'alaea, set back obliquely
to the ocean, is more sheltered. It is more suited to swimming,
while Kawili Beach offers more exciting surfing.

KALUA'AHA CHURCH

East End

An American Congregationalist minister, the Reverend Harvey Rexford Hitchcock, established Moloka'i's first Christian mission here in 1832. He preached to his first converts in a crude thatched hut, though a more permanent church was built in stone a few years later. The white plastering was added in a thoroughgoing restoration in 1917. It fell into disrepair again, and was practically a ruin for several decades before being rebuilt by its congregation (completed 2009). Kalua'aha Church stands beside the Kamehameha V Highway near the island's southern coast, against the rising background of East Moloka'i.

NORTH SHORE PALI

East End

The pali (cliffs) of Moloka'i's north shore are much less famous than those of Kauai's Nā Pali Coast (*see* page 12), but they are every bit as spectacular in their way; more so, perhaps. Rising sheer above the ocean to altitudes of over 1,180 m (3,900 ft) in some places, they are officially the highest sea cliffs in the world. Sublimely harsh as they are, their dramatic impact is only underlined by the way they are counterpointed with lush green valleys, opening up much gentler, softer scenes.

WAIKOLU VALLEY

East End

Just over 1,000 m (3,600 ft) up among the crags of mountainous East Moloka'i, the Waikolu Lookout offers majestic views down one of Moloka'i's most gorgeous valleys to the ocean.

An already exquisite scene is enhanced after rain, when the little streams running down the slopes on either side are swollen, shining silver in the sunlight, and the white surges of countless cataracts appear. The comparative inaccessibility of this area, and its restricted status as part of the Kalaupapa National Historical Park (*see* page 173), has helped to keep this extremely special place unspoiled.

INDEX